AF652451

Cod and Codie Love to Code

Story cum activity book on coding for young children

Story and concept: Dr. Swati Popat Vats

SCHOLASTIC
New York Toronto London Auckland
Sydney New Delhi Hong Kong

Text © 2021 Dr. Swati Popat Vats

All rights reserved.

Published by Scholastic India Pvt. Ltd.
A subsidiary of Scholastic Inc., New York, 10012 (USA).
Publishers since 1920, with international operations in Canada, Australia, New Zealand, the United Kingdom, India, and Hong Kong.

No part of this publication may be reproduced in whole or in part, or stored in a retrieval system, or transmitted in any form or by any means, electronic, mechanical, photocopying, recording, or otherwise without the written permission of the publisher.

For information regarding permission, write to:
Scholastic India Pvt. Ltd.
A-27, Ground Floor, Sigma Centre
Infocity-1, Sector 34, Gurgaon-122001 (India)

First edition: January 2021
This reprint edition: February 2023

ISBN-13: 978-93-90189-75-5

E-book ISBN-13: 978-93-90189-76-2

Printed in India at Saurabh Printers Pvt. Ltd.

Cod and Codie Love to Code

Story cum activity book on coding for young children

Story and concept: Dr. Swati Popat Vats

Activities: Dimple Shah | Manasi Bist
Nisha Thakkar | Henna Ahuja

Design: Purvi J. Mendonca

Dear Parents and Educators,

You must be wondering why a book on coding for young children?

Well, to echo Maria Klawe's famous words, 'Children deserve a chance to become creators instead of consumers of computer science'.

Children are usually put straightaway before the computer screen to learn coding! And our skewed pressure on marks and grades turns their brain into a memory box via rote learning. It's time we changed this; some foundational knowledge is useful before putting children in front of a screen. The aim of this storivity book is to teach kids how to learn, not what to learn. Another important lesson is that we don't listen to gadgets; 'they' listen to us. It is we who have the power over them and not the other way around.

Steve Jobs said, 'Everyone should learn how to code, it teaches you to think.' This preparation must start in an analog form (non-screen). We must first support children to understand coding as a way of life. This book converts everyday activities into sequences, instructions. For e.g.; when we teach children the steps of a task or rules to follow, we are teaching them about ALGORITHMS. Come to think of it, coding is everywhere. When you are giving a step-by-step instruction to someone, when you read instructions of a recipe, or a poem which has the perfect rhyming sequence, when you identify obstacles on the road and avoid them while walking—there is some sort of coding, looping, debugging and so on in every task we do. Any job that you do, you first code your work by creating categories and sequences. You create instructions and debug when you make a mistake. It is all about learning logical thinking and making sense about what it is that you are learning.

Children are exposed to coding from a very early age without them even knowing it! Parenting and coding, both have an 'if-then' approach. The objective is to give children's brains a challenge and have them understand that every choice they make comes with its own consequences. This book will help parents understand children's need for play and tinkering and how this can be connected to later computational thinking skills.

And why should children opt for this book instead of the apps and online courses? We give children screens without helping them understand what their responsibility towards it is. Children should start with computational thinking, not computer-related coding, this is what is missing today. If we start their journey in coding with an abstract tool, the learning will not be beneficial or long lasting. This is the reason why this interactive book is filled with activities that are engaging and impactful.

In this book, Ms. Botty, the robot, cannot do anything unless you code her; this teaches children that we have control over technology. Children should not be taught coding on a computer, without them first learning it practically.

Enjoy this 'storivity' book with your child and give your child, the best foundation in coding for life.

With loads of love,
Dr. Swati Popat Vats

Coding develops computational thinking and computational thinking is nothing but learning to relate, apply and understand.

Here are some coding terms and their connection to everyday learning activities of young children.

1. C oding – is a set of instructions

Listen and follow instructions

- To learn to code effectively and efficiently, you need to learn to follow instructions correctly in order to solve problems and reach your goal.
- Listening and following directions are important skills that span several areas of child development.

2. A lgorithm – is a sequence of codes

- Sequencing is understanding how a series of objects or events occur in a specific and logical order.
- Sequencing activities help to improve logical understanding and reasoning skills in children. Sequencing is one of the most important skills needed to learn to code. Children sequence during block play, singing rhymes or following a routine/timetable.

Sequencing requires two skills—sorting and patterning

a. Sorting

- This is the process or operation of ordering items and data according to specific criteria.
- Sorting and classifying objects helps children begin to notice how items are alike and different, and creates an awareness that is important in learning to code. Sorting objects, colours and shapes are all activities that children do every day.

b. Patterning:

- Encouraging a child's understanding of patterns contributes to the development of various kinds of mathematical thinking, including counting and problem-solving.
- Patterning activities provides a sense of order in what might otherwise appear chaotic and helps to see relationships. It helps children understand, 'what comes before', 'what comes after' and helps them see the continuity in stories, rhymes and everyday activities.

3. D ecomposition – in coding when you decompose a problem or a task, you break it down into smaller tasks.

- When we give instructions to children in steps or when we help them break a task down into steps or when we divide the food on their plate into manageable chunks, we are decomposing a problem or a task!

4. D ebugging – is when you go looking for bugs and errors in your program and fix it to achieve the desired output.

- Activities that help children find out what is missing, or the odd one out, is helping them develop debugging skills!

5. I f-then-else conditionals – helps the program to perform a certain action when faced with choices.

- What would happen if: 'If I want to colour a picture, then I need crayons,' or 'If I want to observe a plant grow, then I need to sow a seed' etc. these are all everyday **If-Then conditionals** that we already expose our children to.

6. L ooping – is a set of instructions in a program or algorithm that are repeated again and again.

- When you add a loop in a sequence you are programming the machine to repeat certain steps to reach the desired output.
- Many nursery rhymes and stories have loops! Like 'Five little ducks went out one day ...' or the story of 'Goldilocks', in both of them the same thing is repeated again and again. These are loops that children are already experiencing in their daily learning activities.

7. P ixel - are the smallest part of a picture

- Pixel activities help improve concentration as it requires one to focus on each and every cell in the grid.
- It helps improve hand-eye coordination and encourages visual analysis.

8. F low charts

- Flow charts help us understand the logical sequence of steps in a program.
- Teaching children about flow charts helps them to learn mind-mapping skills.

9. S orting data variables

- It is necessary for coders to understand that everything has different parts. When different parts are put together it makes a whole and this whole can be broken down into many parts.
- Helping children sort different objects helps them understand similarities and differences, and they are able to do focused observations to sort things into groups. This is also the foundation for venn diagrams.

10. B inary code

- Binary code is a coding system using the binary digits 0 and 1 to represent a letter, digit, or other character in a computer or other electronic device. Computers usually use the binary number system to manipulate and store all of their data including numbers, words, videos, graphics and music.

Introduction to the characters in the story

This is Cod.
He loves to skate, read storybooks and help his parents fix meals. He is often found teaching his pet parrot new words to speak and challenging his twin sister Codie to solve Rubik's Cube puzzles.

This is Codie.
She loves playing music on her piano and doing acrobatics and gymnastics. She is often found engrossed in DIY projects, learning with her mom about computers and playing with her twin brother Cod.

This Cod and Codie's mom.
She is a coder by profession and works in a technology firm. She loves to plan treasure hunts for Cod and Codie where they have to solve puzzles, riddles and codes.

This is Cod and Codie's dad.
He is a football coach and is often found in the backyard devising game plans. He loves to grow organic vegetables and fruits in their garden and playing board games with his friends and family.

This is Ms. Botty.
She is a robot. She was built by Cod and Codie's mom and her team. Cod and Codie love to help their mother program Ms. Botty and use her to help in the household chores and to code her to learn new skills.

This is Red Riding Hood.
She is Cod and Codie's favourite bedtime story character. One day, she comes to meet Cod and Codie. She is planning a birthday party for her friend, Goldilocks, and requests Cod and Codie to help her.

This is Goldilocks.
She is Red Riding Hood's friend. Her friends are having a birthday party for her. She is very excited for the party. She loves solving puzzles.

This is Humpty Dumpty.
He is Goldilocks's friend. He loves solving puzzles just like Goldilocks. He is very excited to attend Goldilocks's birthday party.

They are Hansel and Gretel.
Hansel and Gretel are siblings. They are also Goldilocks's friends. Hansel loves baking and is making a cake for Goldilocks's birthday. Gretel is helping to make buntings for the party decorations.

Meet Cod and Codie. We call them the coding twins. Cod and Codie are very fascinated by the digital world around them.

Their mother is a coder and works for a technology firm. Cod and Codie often hear their mother talk to her office colleagues about coding, codes, programs, algorithms, bugs and lots more.

Cod and Codic enjoy using different electronic and digital devices. Their mother understands the importance of using digital devices safely and has taught them safety rules. The twins always follow the rules set by their parents while using these devices and never exceed the amount of screen time set for them.

Cod and Codie use a screen to talk to their grandparents and to play games.

Sometimes Cod and Codie watch cartoons and sports on television.

Codie likes to solve puzzles and draw pictures on her tablet.

Cod and Codie enjoy finding information on the Internet for their projects, on their computer.

Cod and Codie like to ask questions to Siri and Google Home.

Here are the tech-safety rules that Cod and Codie follow:

1. Don't keep gadgets too close to your eyes. While eating, never play with screens or watch television. Do not use screens one hour before sleep time.

2. Take a break after ten minutes of screen time and do some stretches.

3. Play with toys, books and never use screens for more than one hour a day.

4. Do not view programmes or games with inappropriate language or visuals.

5. Screens are not only for playing games. Always watch screens with an adult around. Tell your parents not to keep their mobile phone in their shirt or pant pocket.

Cod and Codie's mother has taught the twins to code because coding activities are good for the brain and help them develop problem-solving skills and become creative.

Cod and Codie's first interaction with coding was when their mother explained to them that machines can talk like us, walk like us, sing like us and even dance like us.

Their mother introduced them to a robot built by her. Cod and Codie named her Ms. Botty. 'Can Ms. Botty think on her own?' asked Cod and Codie. 'No! Machines cannot think on their own,' said their mother. We have to program the machine, we have to tell the machine what to do using a code. Just like we talk to each other using words and sentences in different languages or use sign language and pictures, computers have their own language called a code.'

Digita

Guess the first letter of each

Literacy

picture to crack the code

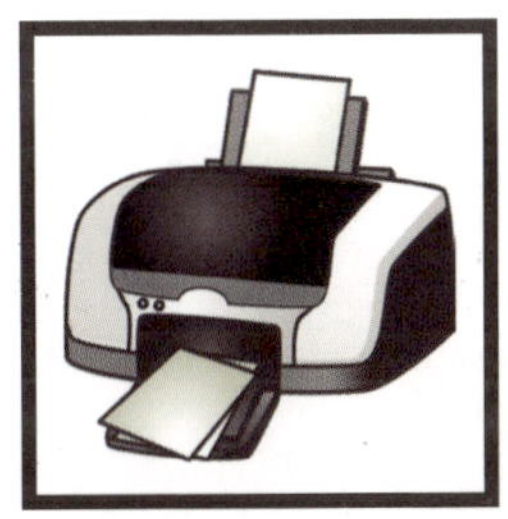

Well done! You can now identify different digital devices around you.

Just like the routine that Cod and Codie follow daily, their mother explained to them that a computer needs a set of instructions to function, this is called a code. The computer needs the instructions in a particular format, like a set or series of steps, this is called an algorithm.

A computer follows everything given in an algorithm, even the mistakes! When the coder makes a mistake in writing the steps of the algorithm, it is called a bug (mistake) and the coder then has to debug, which means to correct the mistake. So a coder has to be very alert and careful not to make mistakes.

Cod and Codie also learnt about good habits from their parents. When they want to have screen time then their mother says, 'if you have eaten your food, then you can watch television' or 'if you are eating, then you cannot play with screens.' Computers also follow 'if-then' codes so that they know what to do and when.

Along with coding, Cod and Codie also love stories and adventures. Their father reads to them wonderful stories from a beautiful storybook. Their teacher tells them interesting stories in school and they watch fascinating tales on television too.

Here are their favourite storybook characters. Can you help them join the storybook characters to their related objects.

Well done!

One day, as Cod and Codie opened their storybook, a girl waved out to them. 'Hi, Cod and Codie,' she said. 'Welcome to Storyland.'

The twins were very surprised. 'How do you know us, Red Riding Hood?' they asked her.

'Just as you know me,' she replied. 'I see you peering into my story pages so often.

‘There is a pattern you follow each time. You first go to the contents page, you read the names of the stories in the book, then you check the page number of the story you want to read and turn the pages to reach that page number. I am so happy each time you come to my story.’

‘Yes, Red Riding Hood, we love to follow a sequence because we love coding. But you look sad today, is something the matter?’ Codie and Cod asked.

Sequencing

Write numbers 1, 2, 3, 4, 5 or 6 in the boxes below each picture to put them in the correct sequence.

sprout

water

soil

sunlight

plant

seeds

Sequencing

Write numbers 1, 2, 3, 4, 5 or 6 in the boxes below each picture to put them in the correct sequence.

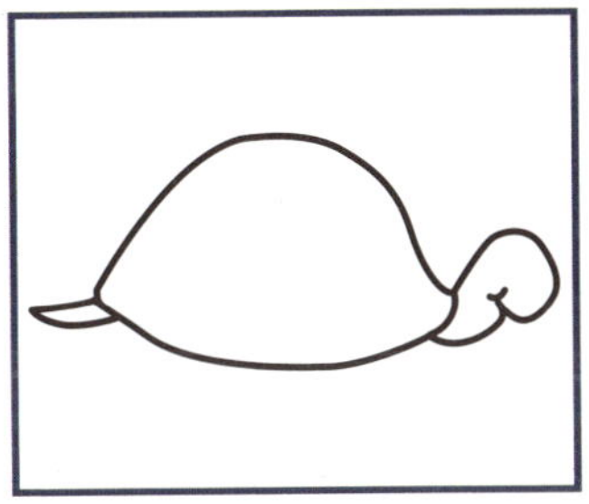

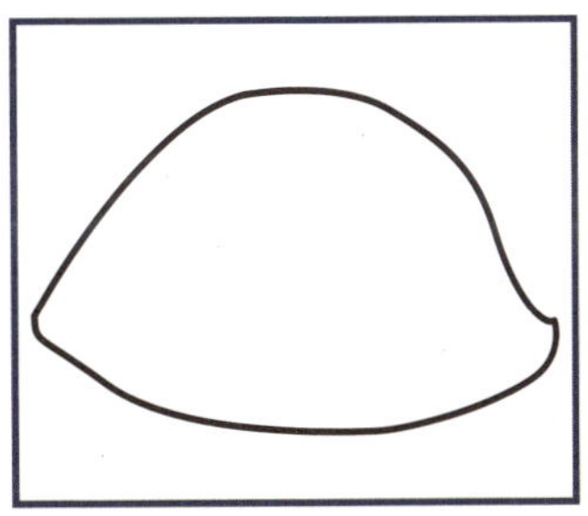

Good job! You are now ready for other coding activities.

'Oh, I have a problem,' Red Riding Hood told Cod and Codie.

'I am having a surprise birthday party in the evening for my friend Goldilocks. There are so many preparations to be done. I have to clean my room, put up decorations, bake a cake and make sandwiches for everyone. I also have to plan a surprise gift for Goldilocks. So many things to do and so little time. Please, can you help me? I don't know where to begin.'

'Of course, we can,' Cod and Codie assured her. 'Let's begin with tidying up your room Ms. Botty our robot can help you with that.'

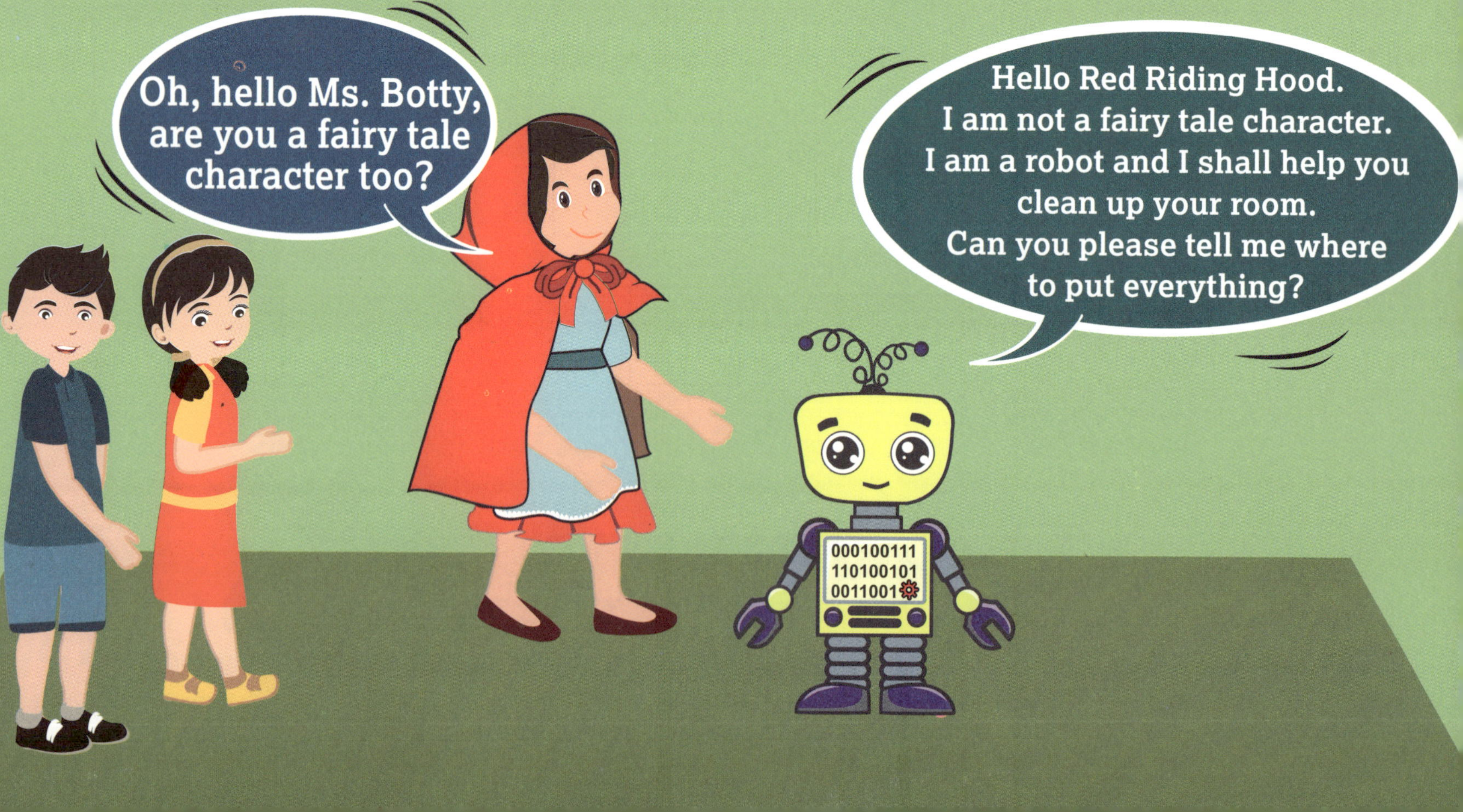

Following instructions

Try this activity with your parent or friend.
One of you can give instructions and the other has to follow the instructions.

1 Jump 10 times

Stop

2 Twist your hips twice

Stop

3 Stand straight

4 Hop 5 times on your left foot

Stop

5 Hop 5 times on your right foot

Stop

6 Squat 5 times

Stop

7 Duck walk for 10 steps

Stop

8 Touch your toes

Stop

9 Stand up straight

Stop

Cod told Red Riding Hood that Ms. Botty would only be able to follow instructions and complete the task correctly when we gave her specific instructions. Here is an example.

'Ms. Botty, please jump.' Ms. Botty starts jumping non-stop.

Enter the room
↓
Walk towards the toys
↓
Pick them up
↓
Walk towards the toy box
↓
Put the toys in the toy box
↓
Walk towards the pile of clothes
↓
Pick up the pile of clothes
↓
Put the clothes in the laundry basket
↓
Stop

Codie told Ms. Botty to stop and gave her another instruction. 'Ms. Botty, hop on your left foot three times and then stop.' Ms. Botty hopped on her left foot one, two and three times and then stopped.
Cod and Codie made a list of steps—called an algorithm—for Ms. Botty to follow to clean the room.
Algorithm is a list of steps that tells you precisely what steps to take to reach your goal.

Let's try an Alogrithm activity

Which algorithm will take you to the school safely?

Home

Get into the school bus 

↓

Sit properly on your seat 

↓

Do not put your hand out of the window 

↓

Do not run in the bus 

↓

Get down at the school gate 

School

Home

Get into the school bus 

↓

Run around the bus 

↓

Put your head and hand outside the bus 

↓

Sit properly in the bus 

↓

Get down 

School

Good job! You now understand algorithms.

Soon, all the toys had been picked up and kept away tidily by Ms. Botty. Red Riding Hood was very excited for Goldilocks's birthday party. She had made special cards to invite all her friends to the party. She gave one to Cod and Codie too.

'Oh! Red Riding Hood, how will all your friends know how to reach the birthday party? There are no directions to reach the house. Let's make a map with algorithm (steps) that will help all your friends reach the party,' said Cod.

'Yes, that's a great idea,' said Red Riding Hood.

Humpty Dumpty was also invited to the birthday party. But he lived in a kingdom far away from Red Riding Hood's house.

They decided to make a special map for Humpty Dumpty so that he could avoid all the obstacles on his way and reach the party safely, without having a great fall!

Red Riding Hood thanked Cod and Codie for making all the maps for her friends.

Let's try another Alogrithm activity

Look at this map for Humpty Dumpty, and notice the arrow positions. Now look at the three route options given. Circle the correct route option.

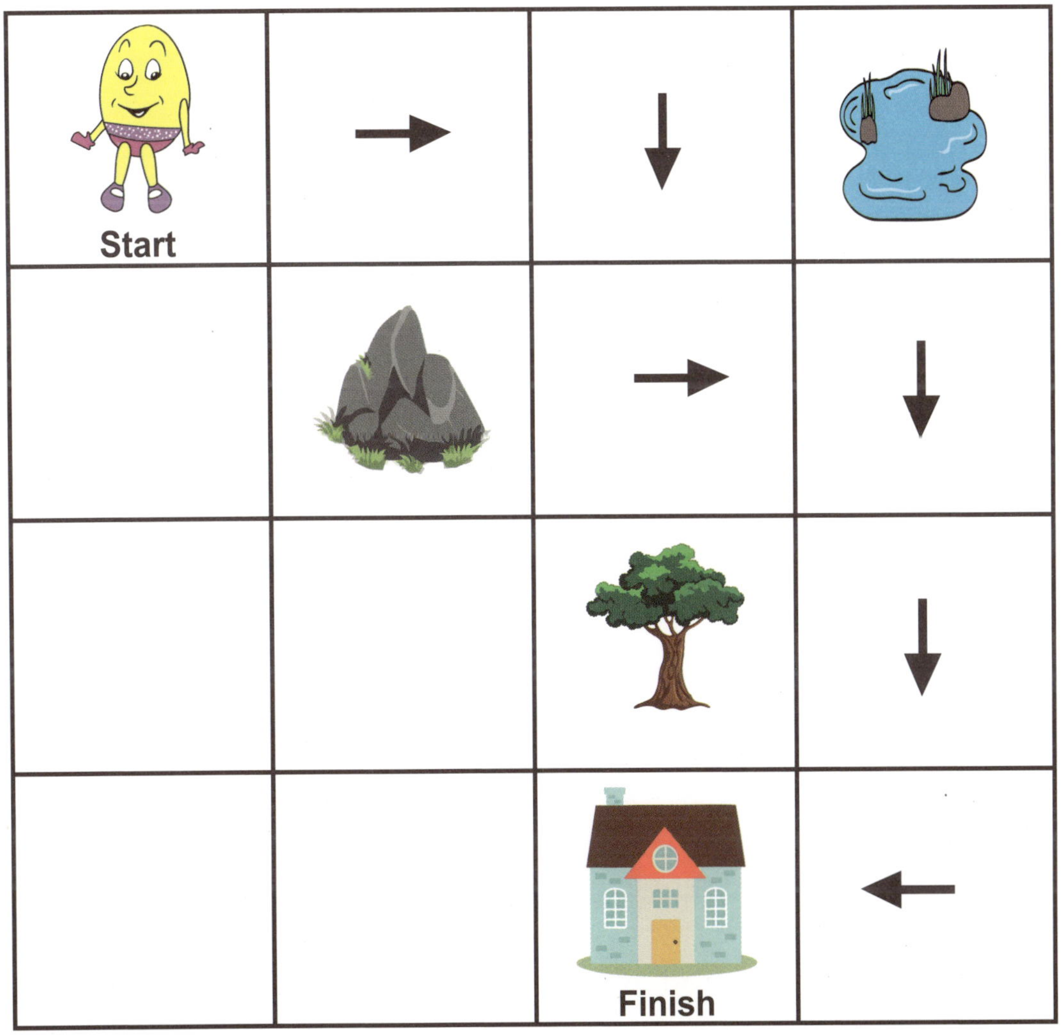

1st Route → ↑ ↓ ←

2nd Route → ↑ ↓ ← ↑

3rd Route → ↓ → ↓ ↓ ←

Try this Alogrithm activity

Each of these algorithms has one or more errors. Rewrite the code that works so that Ms. Botty can walk from the start point to the finish point by avoiding the obstacle.

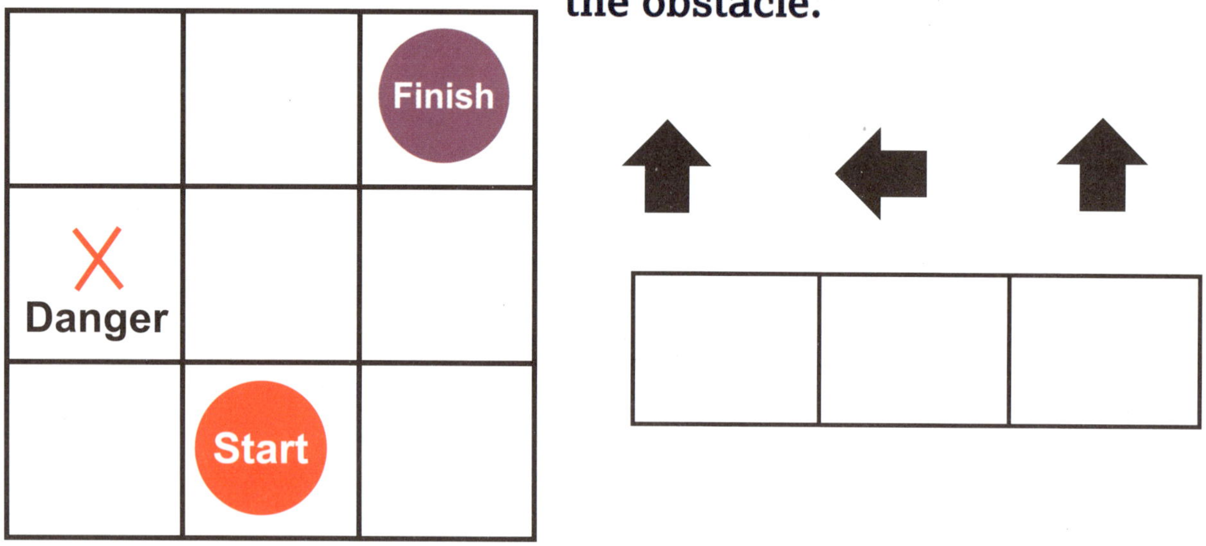

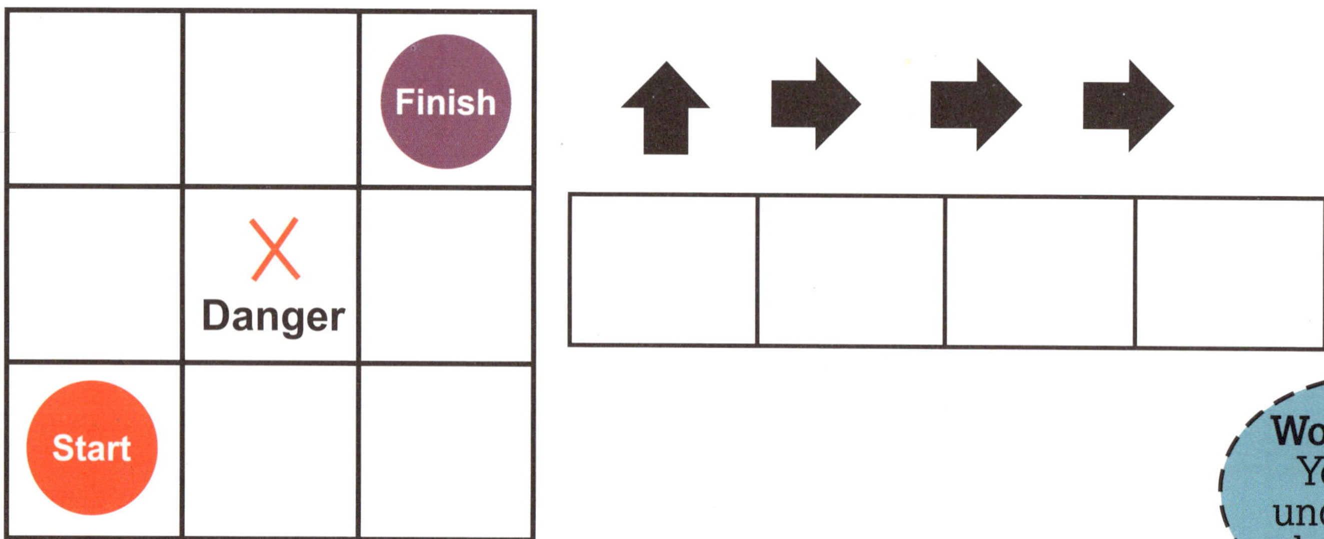

Codes

Move Up	Move Down	Move Right	Move Left
↑	↓	→	←

Here is another Alogrithm activity

Cod and Codie are trying to code Ms. Botty to walk around the room and help them pack their school bag. Write the algorithm using the codes given at the bottom of this page in the sequence you want Ms. Botty to follow. Draw the path in the grid below to check the sequence of your algorithm.

Sequence: 1. School Bag 2. Pencil box 3. Books 4. Tiffin box 5. Water

Codes

Move Up	Move Down	Move Right	Move Left	Get Item
⬆	⬇	➡	⬅	☺

Soon Hansel and Gretel arrived at the birthday party. Now it was time for them to decorate the room for the party. Gretel suggested that they decorate the room with bunting of different colours. Red Riding Hood brought sheets of different coloured paper, scissors and strings to make the bunting.

As they needed to decorate the whole room with buntings, Codie suggested that they break up this task. Their mother had taught them that in coding a big task is broken up into smaller tasks, it is called decompose. They each took up one sheet of coloured paper. They folded it, drew a shape on it and cut out the pattern to make buntings of different shapes.

Decomposition - breaking down into parts

Match the whole to its parts.

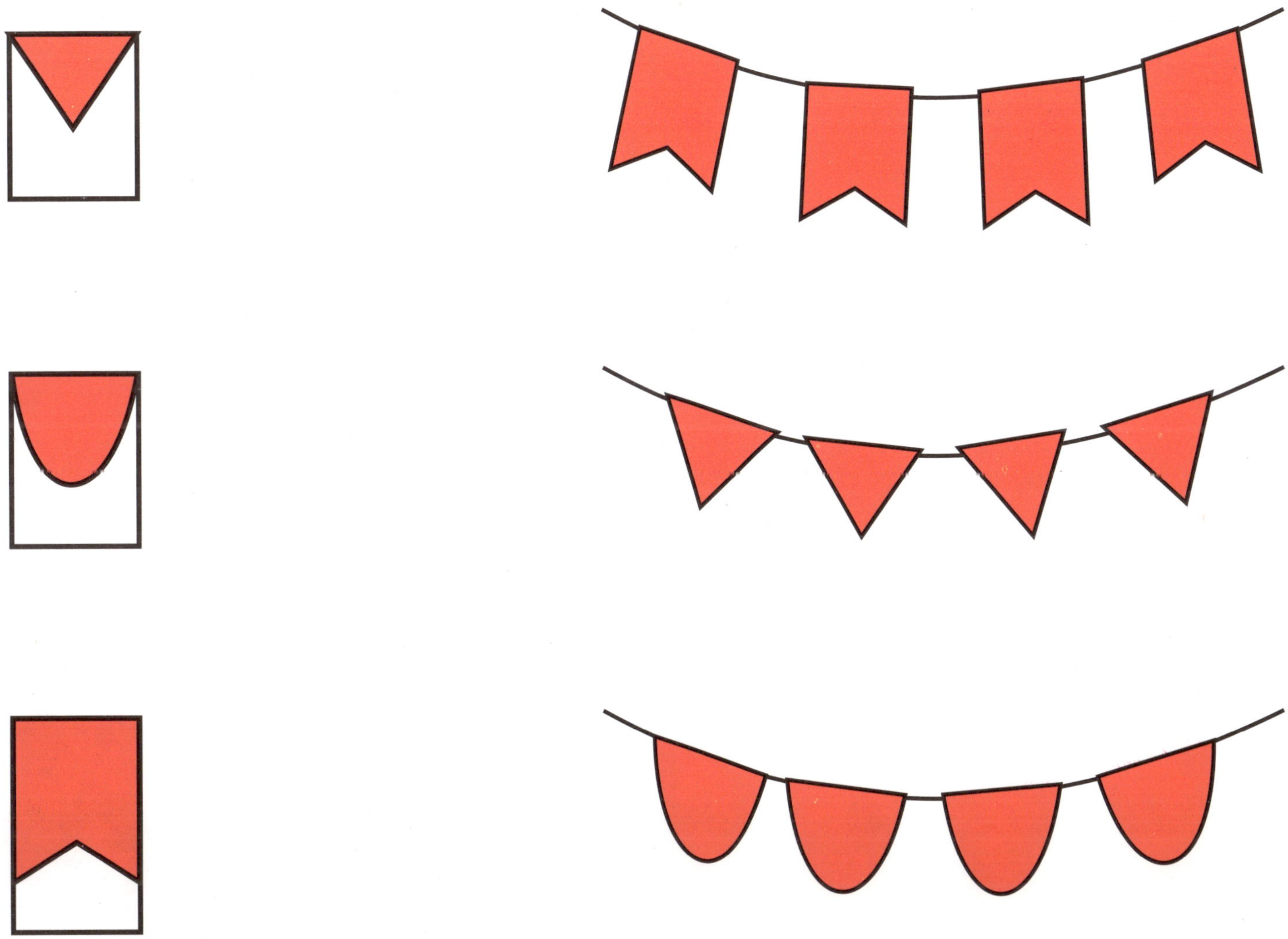

A birthday party is incomplete without a birthday cake. Hansel loved baking cakes and was going to make Goldilocks's favourite chocolate cake for her birthday. He got all the ingredients he would need to make the cake. Hansel followed his dad's special recipe and put the cake in the oven to bake.

When the timer on the oven went off, Hansel excitedly took the cake out of the oven. He cut a small piece of the cake to check it's taste. He was shocked as the chocolate cake was sour. 'Oh no!' he screamed.

Cod and Codie came running to the kitchen to see what had happened. Hansel told them that the cake tasted sour and he did not know what had gone wrong with it.

Cod and Codie smiled at his confusion and explained to him that in computer language a mistake is a bug, so they will now debug his recipe, by finding the mistake.

Debugging

Find the bug/mistake in the steps of the cake recipe.

Ingredients

- 1 cup of flour
- 1 egg
- 1 cup of sugar
- 2 tablespoons of cocoa
- 2 cups of milk
- 1 cup of chocolate syrup

Crack the eggs carefully

Put tamarind in the bowl

Put cocoa in the bowl

Pour milk, flour and sugar in the bowl

Mix for 2 minutes

Place in the oven

Cake is ready!

Well done! You can now debug.

Debugging

All the animals want to reach their home, but one animal in each picture is going the wrong way (mistake/bug). Circle the bug/mistake in each picture.

Hansel was relieved once the bug in the cake recipe was identified and debugged.

Now it was time for Gretel to make sandwiches for everyone at the party. She had very little time to make the sandwiches. She decided to call Ms. Botty and ask for her help.

Gretel gave Ms. Botty all the ingredients that she would need to make the sandwiches. She also explained the steps that she would have to follow to make the sandwiches.

Ms. Botty made a sandwich to show Gretel.

But there were so many more sandwiches to be made. This would take a lot of time. 'I cannot keep giving the same instructions to Ms. Botty as I have other things to do,' said Gretel.

Codie heard this and suggested, 'Gretel, why don't we put the instructions in a loop for Ms. Botty! A loop means putting the same instructions in a repeat format, this will help Ms. Botty repeat the same set of instructions many times.'

Looping

The 'Hokey Pokey' song uses a loop with a different part of the body each time. Sing the song and do the actions each time you go round the loop.

You put your right hand in,
You put your right hand out,
You put your right hand in,
And you shake it all about.
You do the Hokey Pokey,
And you turn around,
That's what it's all about.

You put your left hand in,
You put your left hand out,
You put your left hand in,
And you shake it all about.
You do the Hokey Pokey,
And you turn around,
That's what it's all about.

You put your right foot in,
You put your right foot out,
You put your right foot in,
And you shake it all about.
You do the Hokey Pokey,
And you turn around,
That's what it's all about.

You put your left foot in,
You put your left foot out,
You put your left foot in,
And you shake it all about.
You do the Hokey Pokey,
And you turn around,
That's what it's all about.

You put your whole self in,
You put your whole self out,
You put your whole self in
And you shake it all about.
You do the Hokey Pokey,
And you turn around,
That's what it's all about.

It was finally time for the party. Goldilocks reached Red Riding Hood's house. She tried opening the door, but it wouldn't open. She tried looking for the bell but she couldn't find it. As she knocked on the door, a picture appeared on it. There were many shapes in the picture.

Goldilocks heard a voice:

Hello, Goldilocks. Welcome to your birthday party. You have to identify the pattern and complete it to open the door and enter the party!

Patterning

Help Goldilocks open the door by completing the pattern in each row.

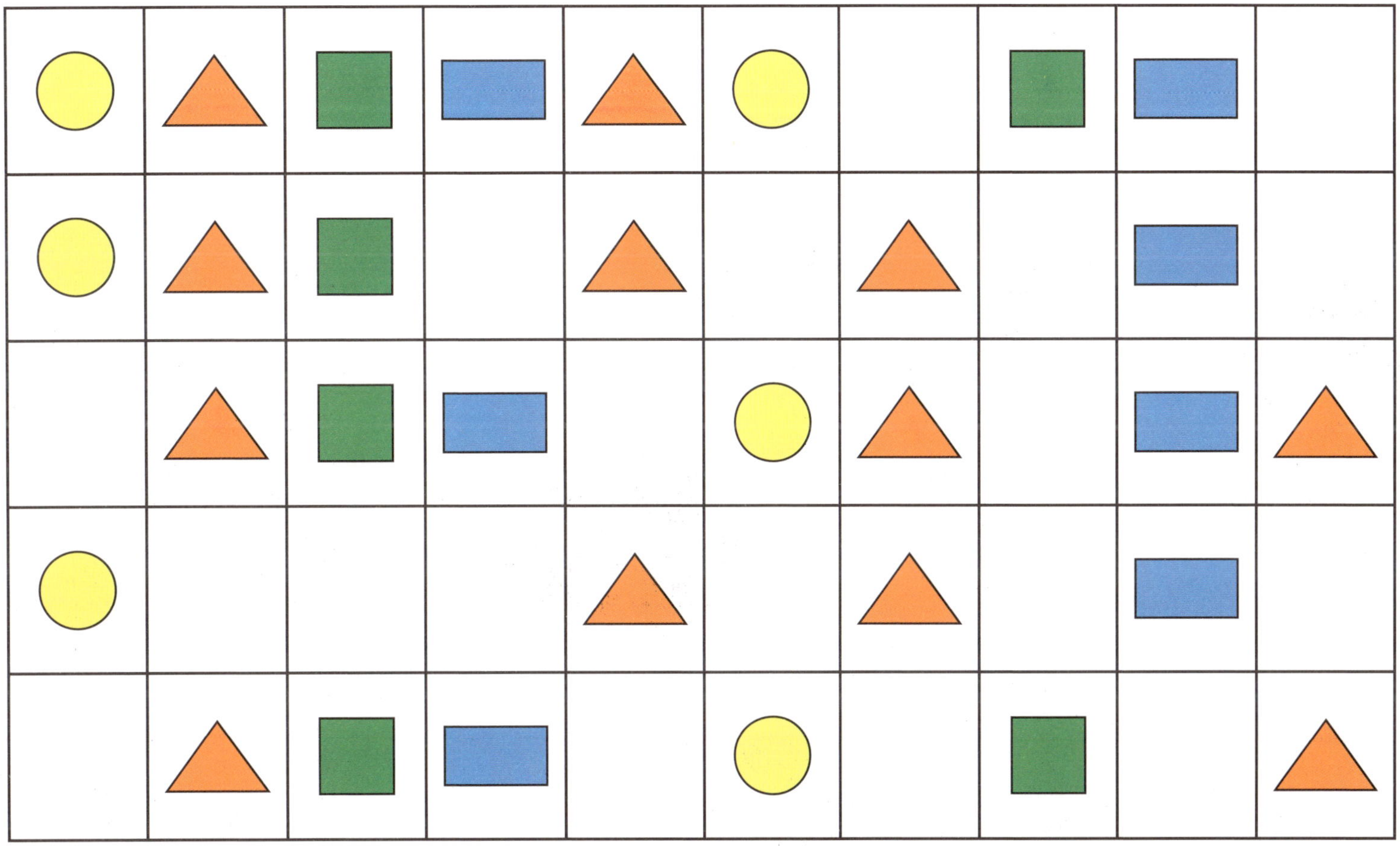

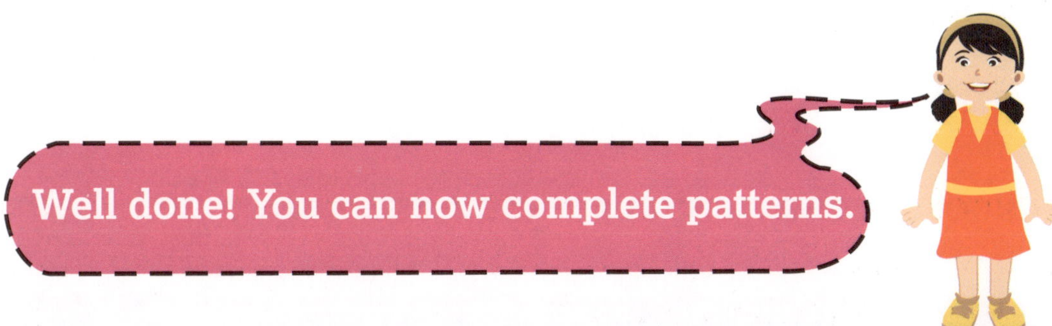

Golidlocks was happy to see all the arrangements. Cod and Codie announced that if everyone at the party was hungry, then they could start eating the snacks, else they could play games.

Flowchart

Follow the flow chart to move to the next activity.

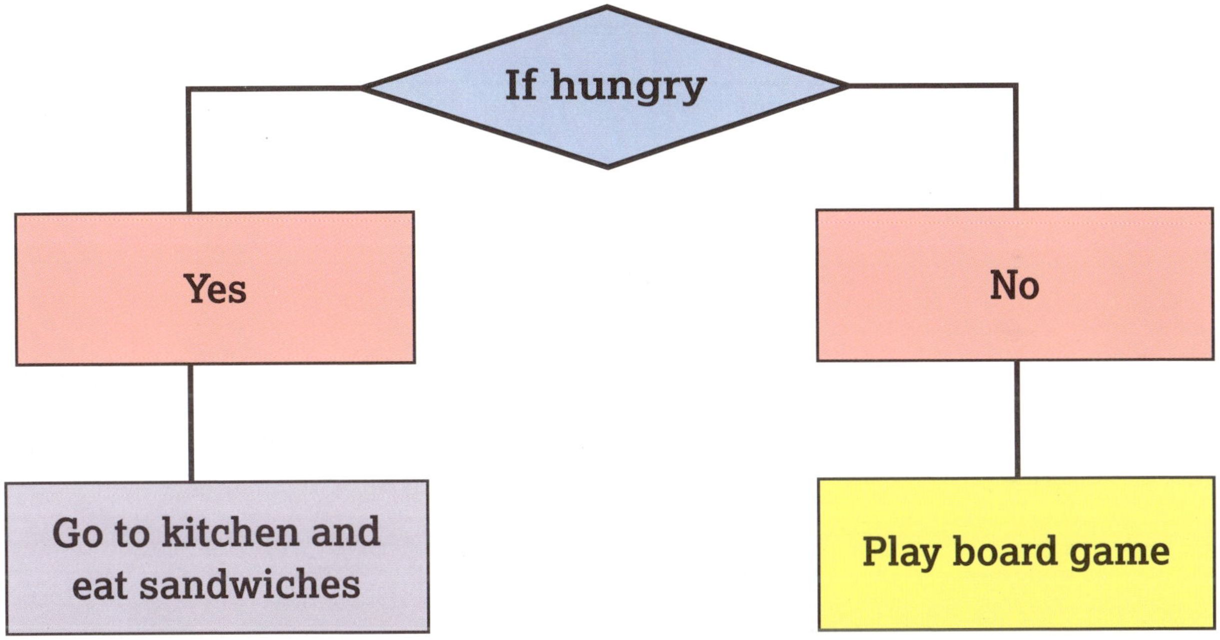

Take help from an adult and create your flow chart.

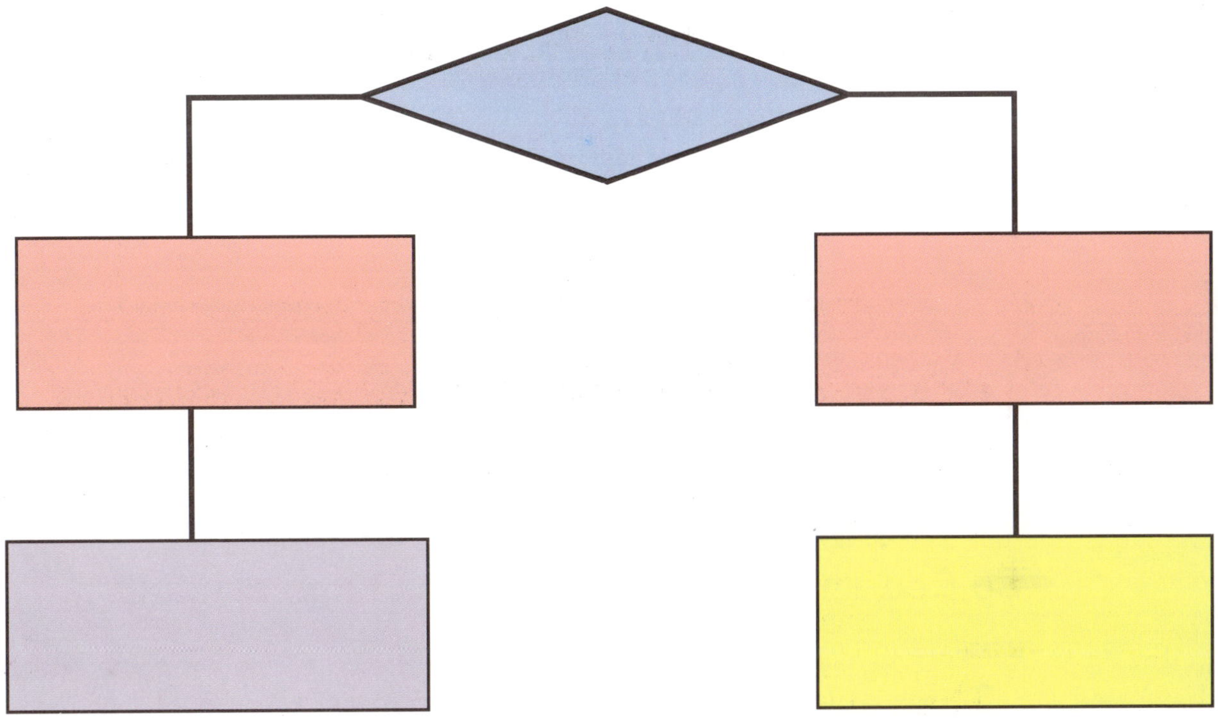

All the friends decided that they wanted to play games first and then have snacks.
So Cod and Codie brought out a huge mat and put it on the floor.
They asked everyone to sit around the mat.
They explained the rules of the game to everyone.

If-then-else

Let's play this 'if-then-else' game. Roll a dice. Check the number on the dice. Move that many steps on the path given below.
If it is a three-letter word, then move two steps ahead.
If it is a two-letter word, then skip the next turn.
If it is a four-letter word, then you get another turn.

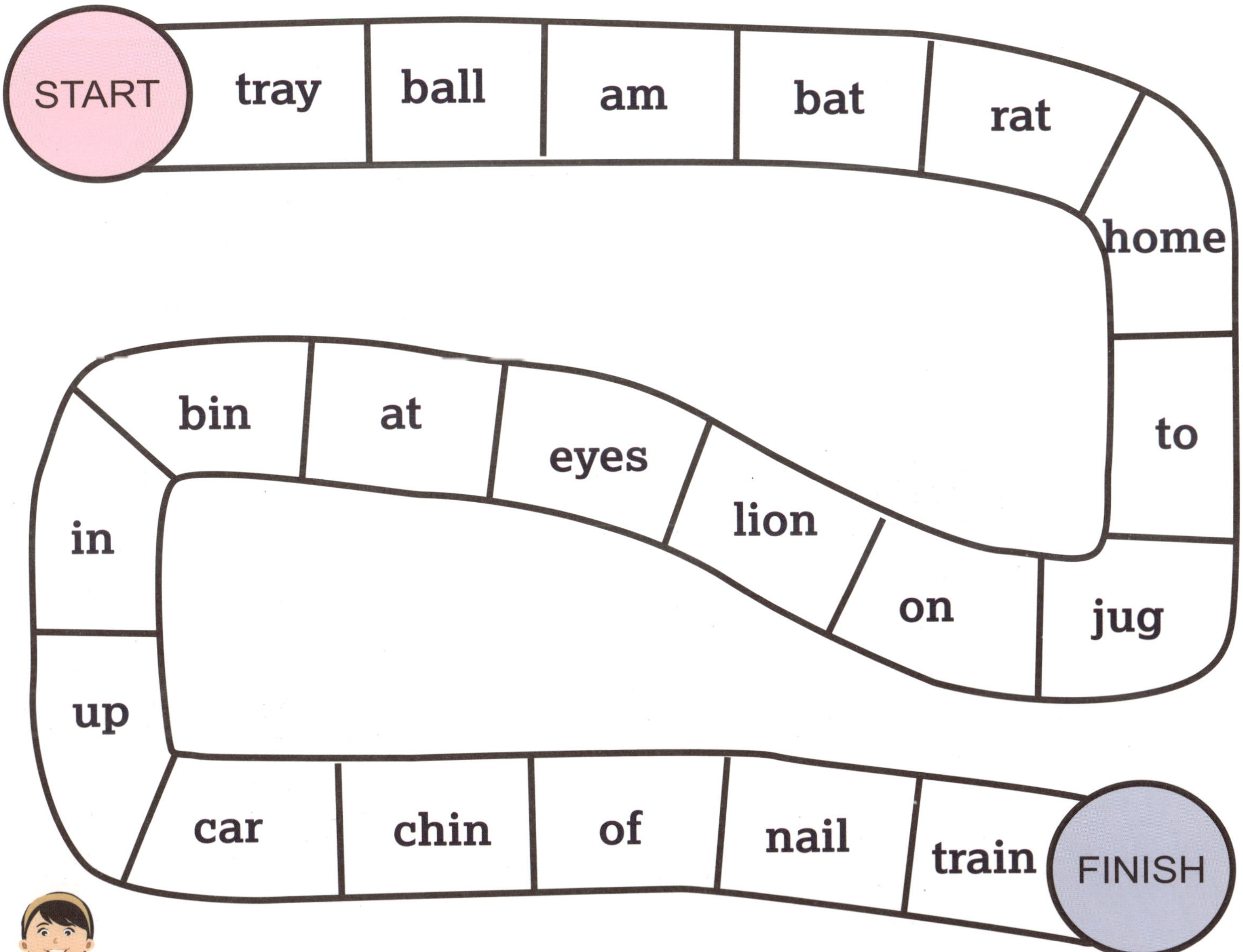

Well done! You can now understand 'If-then-else' conditions.

Codie said, ‘Hello, everybody! It is time to dance and we are going to do the birdie dance. Are you all ready?’

Algorithm

Birdie Dance Algorithm

Follow the algorithm (steps) given below to do the birdie dance.

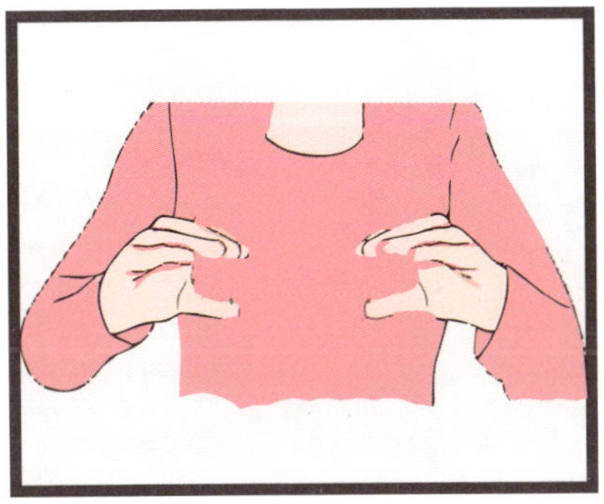

Touch your fingertips

Flap your arms like wings

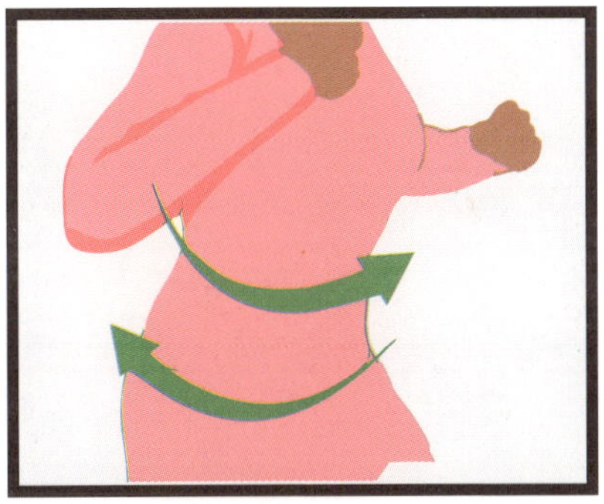

Then you shake your hips

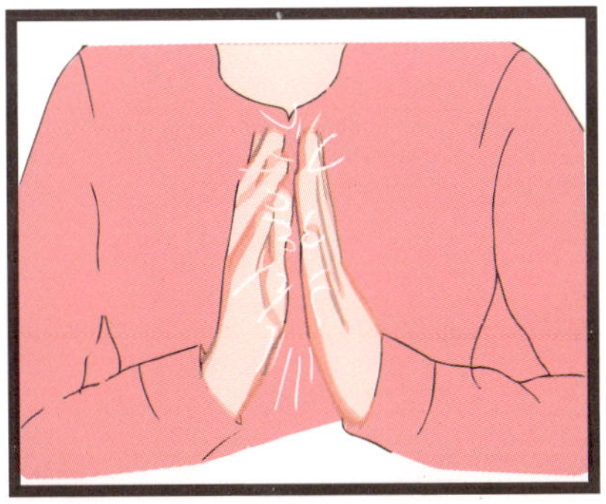

And clap clap clap your hands

Repeat and Loop

It was now time for Goldilocks to blow the candles and cut the cake. Everyone gathered around the cake to sing the birthday song for Goldilocks. Everyone relished the cake made by Hansel and the yummy sandwiches made by Gretel and Ms. Botty.

Goldilocks was eagerly waiting to open her birthday presents. But her friends had planned a surprise for her. They had hidden all the presents in a special place. They gave Goldilocks a piece of paper that had a unique riddle with a code on it. The code would lead her to her presents. Cod and Codie had prepared this really cool coded riddle. Goldilocks began her quest for her presents.

Decoding

Hello Goldilocks, decode the riddle given below to reach the gifts.

Walk up the 

Go to the 

Look under the 

You will see the 

Untie the 

Open the 

You will find your surprise gifts.

'Great! Bravo! Hurray!' shouted all the friends. Goldilocks was able to break the code and reach her presents which were hidden under the bed. She was surprised to see that all her friends had also made coding quests for her to solve in order to open the gifts.

Hansel and Gretel's gift had a special kind of pattern on it. Goldilocks needed to identify what was missing in the pattern and complete it to open the gift.

Spot the pattern

Look at the pattern on each side of the cube and complete it.

Goldilocks successfully solved the pattern and was able to open Hansel and Gretel's gift. The next gift was from Humpty Dumpty and he too had created a puzzle.

The gift had a grid and Goldilocks needed to arrange the butterflies in each row to match the arrow given above. Cod and Codie had helped him create this pattern, it is called matching variables (matching similar objects, patterns).

Sorting Data Variable

Sort and place the butterflies in the grid below as per their colour and the direction they are flying in.

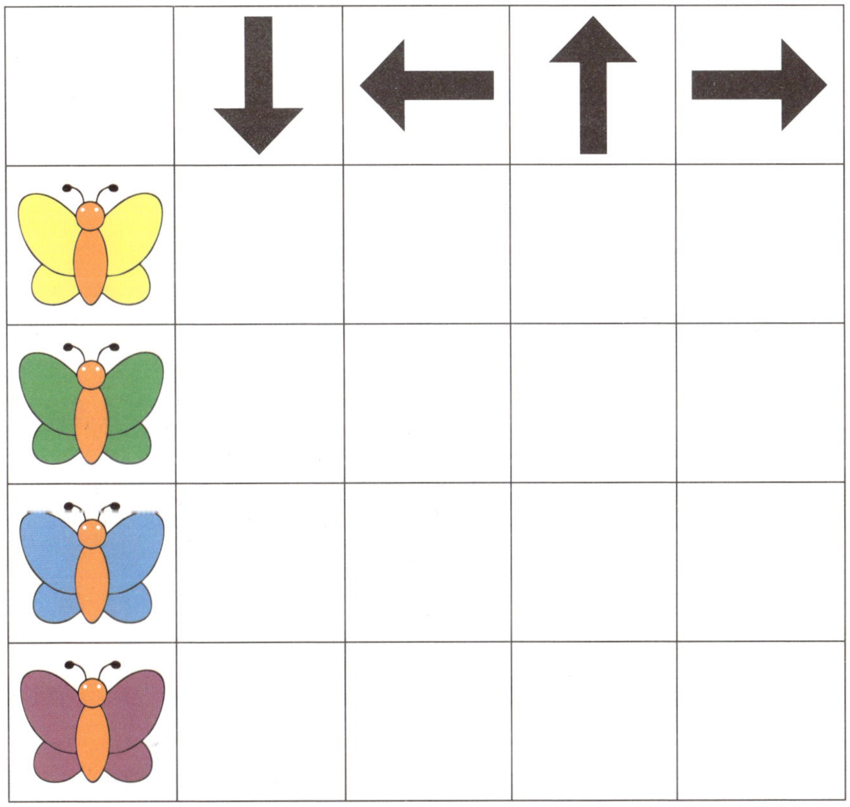

Everybody clapped and cheered for Goldilocks as she sorted the variables and completed the pattern. The final gift was from Red Riding Hood. Her gift was wrapped in a sheet of paper with tiny numbered squares (pixels) on it. Goldilocks had to colour the squares as per the code given to unwrap her present.

Pixels

Look at the colour given for each number. Colour the pixels (boxes) to reveal the image.

1=   **2=**   **3=**   **4=**

		2	2				2	2		
		2		2		2		2		
			2	2	2	2	2			
		1	1	1	3	1	1	1		
		1	1	1	3	1	1	1		
		4	4	4	3	4	4	4		
		1	1	1	3	1	1	1		
		1	1	1	3	1	1	1		

Good job!
You can now
understand pixels.

Finally, Goldilocks was able to break the codes and open all her presents. She thanked her friends for planning this wonderful birthday party for her.

All the fairy tale characters—Red Riding Hood, Goldilocks, Hansel and Gretel, and Humpty Dumpty—thanked Cod and Codie for teaching them fun and interesting coding skills.

Red Riding Hood looked at Ms. Botty and asked, 'What is this peculiar design on Ms. Botty? Does it mean anything?'

'It's her name written in binary code!' replied Cod and Codie.

Red Riding Hood asked, 'What is binary code?'

Cod and Codie replied, 'Binary code is a code language of a computer. Come! We will teach you how to write your names in binary code.'

Everyone then tried writing their names in binary code. Cod and Codie also taught a special handshake to their friends. They all had fun doing the special handshake and promised to greet each other with this handshake every time they met.

Binary Code Your Name

Write each letter of your name in the spaces (_____) given below. Follow the code on the left side of the page to then write your name in binary code in the boxes given on the right.

Lower Case	
a	01100001
b	01100010
c	01100011
d	01100100
e	01100101
f	01100110
g	01100111
h	01101000
i	01101001
j	01101010
k	01101011
l	01101100
m	01101101
n	01101110
o	01101111
p	01110000
q	01110001
r	01110010
s	01110011
t	01110100
u	01110101
v	01110110
w	01110111
x	01111000
y	01111001
z	01111010

Upper Case	
A	01000001
B	01000010
C	01000011
D	01000100
E	01000101
F	01000110
G	01000111
H	01001000
I	01001001
J	01001010
K	01001011
L	01001100
M	01001101
N	01001110
O	01001111
P	01010000
Q	01010001
R	01010010
S	01010011
T	01010100
U	01010101
V	01010110
W	01010111
X	01011000
Y	01011001
Z	01011010

(Write your name here)

_____

_____

_____

_____

_____

_____

_____

_____

_____

_____

Algorithm

Follow the steps given below to do the handshake algorithm with your friend.

1

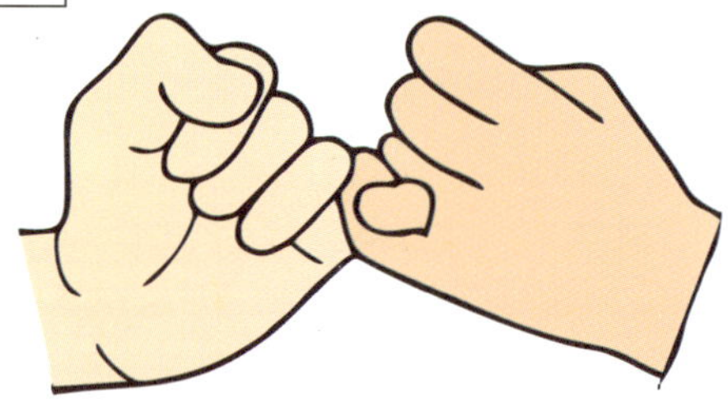

2

3

4

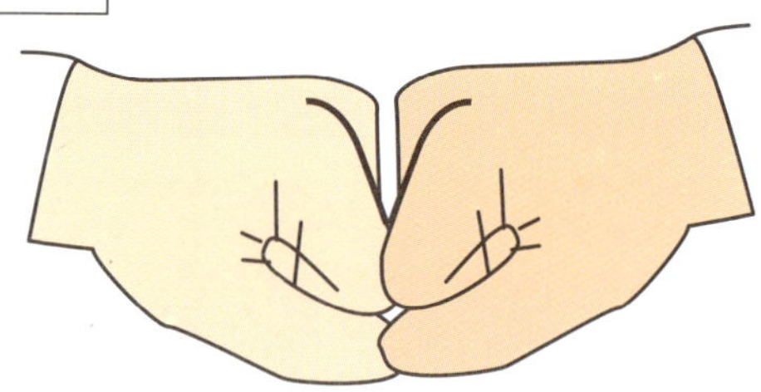

5

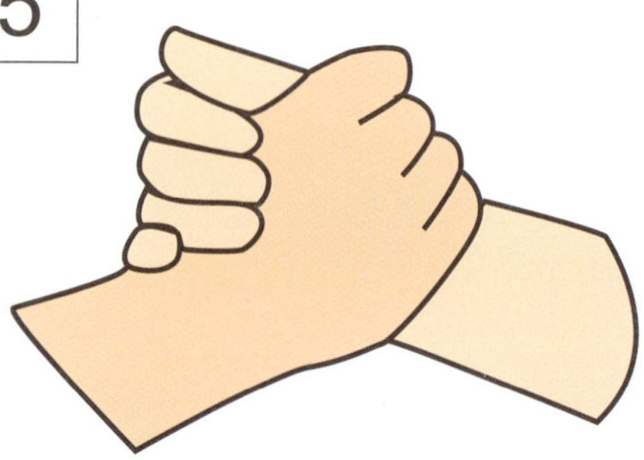

I have started coding with Cod and Codie

Children learnt the basic principles of coding through this story and many fun activities. The various elements of coding are explained simply for a child to follow.

By exposing children early to coding skills, we help them develop various competencies. Children learn an array of skills that make them equipped and ready for the technology-driven world.

1

I can sequence ...
I learnt to sequence through activities involving my daily routine.

2

I can spot and create patterns ...
I now understand that pattern is an arrangement of things that repeat in a logical way. Through worksheets, I am now able to spot and create patterns.

3

Because I can pattern and sequence, I can now understand algorithms ...
I learnt to give and follow specific instructions in sequential steps. I now understand algorithms through various activities on maps, a dance routine and handshake algorithm.

4

I can decompose ...
I learnt to decompose (break down) complex tasks into smaller steps through paper folding and cutting activities and matching the whole picture to its parts.

5

I can debug ...
I learnt to identify errors (bugs) through worksheets and activities.

6

I can loop ...
I understand the concept of looping (repeat again and again) through songs and rhymes.

7

I can sort variables ...
I understand that the same object can be sorted in different ways by changing its variables.

8

I can use conditionals ...
Conditionals help me to understand if I have to perform an action or not. This is dependent on whether the statement is true or false. I learnt to use conditionals by playing If-Then-Else board games and creating flowcharts.

9

I can understand pixels ...
I revealed a hidden image by coloring boxes (pixels) on it, to understand that an image is made of many pixels. Activities involving pixels improve concentration as they require to focus on each and every square in the grid.

10

I can code ...
I have developed a basic set of coding skills like sequencing, patterning, decomposing, debugging, creating algorithms, looping, sorting data variables, using conditionals and am now ready to begin coding robots.

Answer Key

Page 12

Jack - Beanstalk
Humpty Dumpty - Wall
Hansel and Gretel - Chocolate house
Red Riding Hood - Basket
Goldilocks - Porridge

Page 15
Page 16

5-3-1-4-6-2

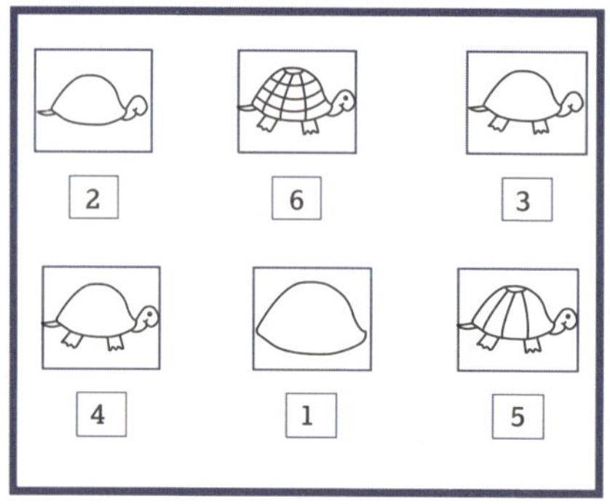

2-6-3-4-1-5

Page 20 1st algorithm

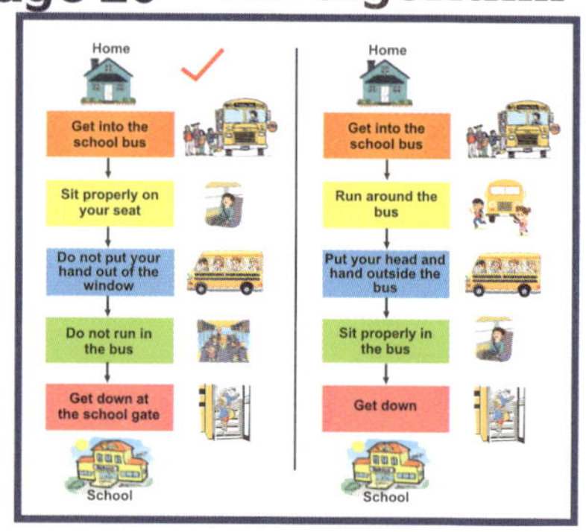

Page 24
3rd Route

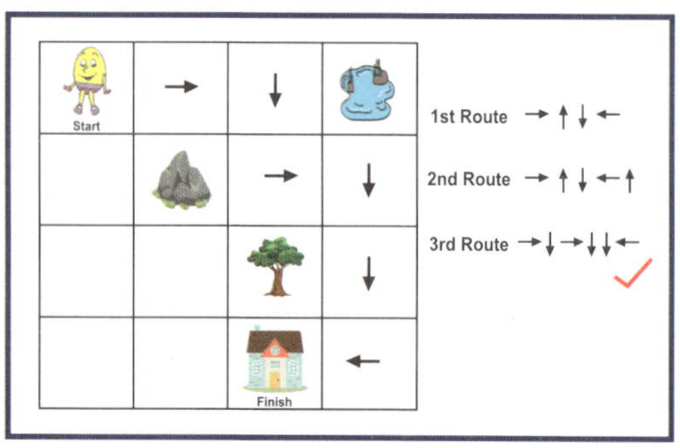

Page 25

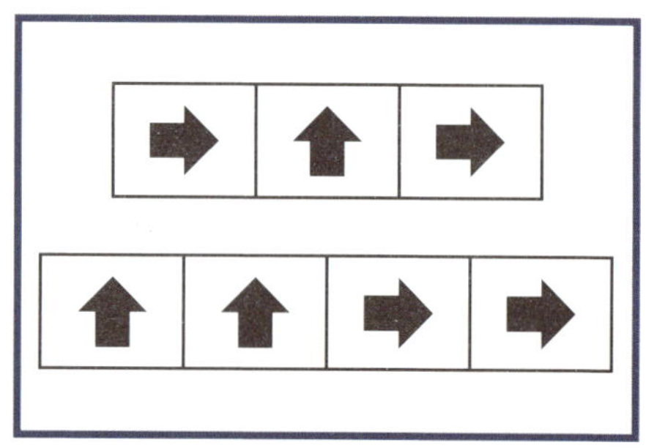

Page 26

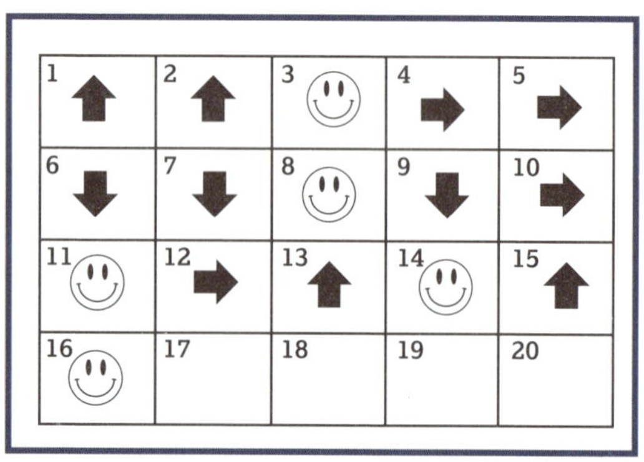

Page 28

1-b
2-c
3-a

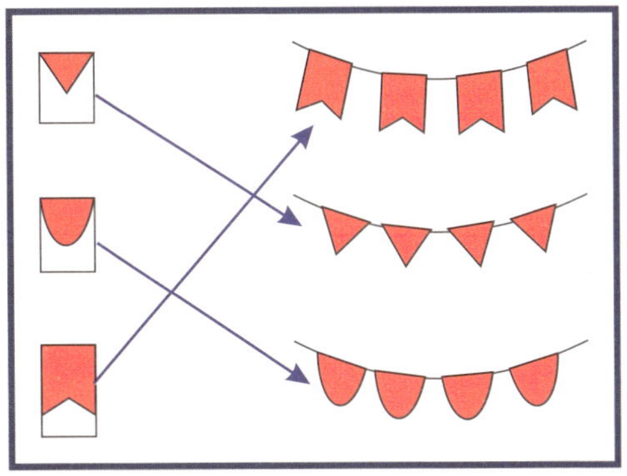

Page 31

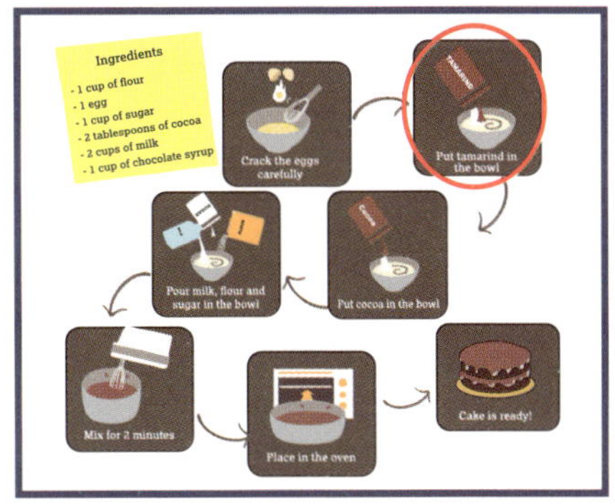

Page 32

Bee facing downward

Front facing duck

Monkey coming down the tree

Ant going down the ant hill

Page 40

Page 50

Page 52

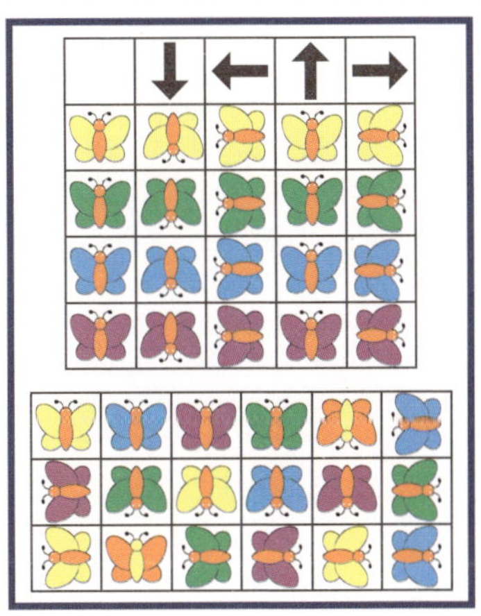

Page 54

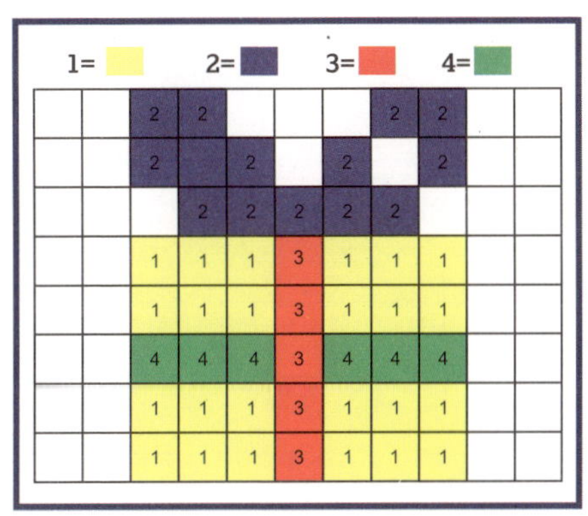

A-Z of Coding

Read, find out and learn ...

a Algorithm	**b** BASIC	**c** Computational thinking, C++,C#	**d** Debugging	**e** Education of coding
f Fortran	**g** Gender neutral	**h** Hacking	**i** If-Then-Else (conditionals)	**j** Java, JavaScript
k KRYPTON	**l** Looping	**m** MAD (Michigan Algorithm Decoder)	**n** Nanotechnology	**o** Open source
p Python	**q** Queue	**r** Robots	**s** ScratchJr.	**t** Tynker
u Usability	**v** Virus	**w** Women in coding	**x** X++	**y** Yes I love coding!
		z Zeroes and Ones		

About the author

Swati is a born tinkerer! She was a hyperactive child who enjoyed boisterous play and experimenting with objects and gadgets. Now, she designs curriculums that help children tinker and help adults understand how to harness a child's learning capacity. With over three decades of experience as an educator, Swati is on the global think tank team of Kidzania and is the president of Early Childhood Association. She has designed the world's first curriculum for coding for early years and over 45,000 children are presently using it at 500 Podar Jumbo Kids kindergartens! She has included activities like Froebel gifts, readiness games, listening and instruction games and puppetry to help children learn to understand coding as she believes that coding will help children's brains understand how to learn and not just what to learn!

She has authored a coding book for four to six year olds titled *'Yash and Yashika learn about Coding'*, also published by Scholastic.

ALSO BY THE AUTHOR